TERMINATE DEBT

The Definitive Guide to Fast Track your Future and
Achieve Financial Freedom

Curtis Carmichael

TERMINATE DEBT

Published by Apollo Ventures LLC, Nashua, New Hampshire.
Category: Wealth Management
ISBN: 9798702592077

DEDICATION

To Rachael, for her support and encouragement in helping me write this book.

To my family for their support and feedback.

And to everyone else in their pursuit of true financial freedom and the 'American Dream': I wish you the very best and hope this book helps you along the way.

TERMINATE DEBT

TABLE OF CONTENTS

INTRODUCTION

MY FORMER SITUATION WAS LIKE MANY OTHERS

In my younger years post-college, like many others starting in the 'real world', I ended up becoming in debt with no end in sight.

The cycle usually begins with a low-paying, entry-level job (due to less experience), and expensive monthly utility bills, student loans, car payments, and any other bills one has. For me, that also included credit card payments, and a bank loan.

Many struggle to stay 'above water', including myself. It was not until much later that I was able to make substantial, lasting improvements to pay off debt.

I took pride in managing my debt, and I owned my situation. I understood that in time, things would improve. I also knew that once my debt was under control, I could start saving money, and make retirement and other investment contributions.

Even though I felt I had it bad, I know that many others were in a worse situation. Debt issues come at any age. Some might come into debt when they need to care for a family member, pay off an estate, start over after a divorce, experience health issues with costs not covered (or fully covered) by insurance, needing to pay for expenses with their kids, etc. It may also entail paying off costs from an unsuccessful business, unexpected costs such as needing to repair a leaking roof or replace a furnace or water heater. The possibilities of debt are endless – some that we can control, and others that we cannot.

Today, after years of perseverance and focus, I now have a positive net worth, and have minimal debt outside of a mortgage and student loans. This was not an easy achievement, and it still requires self-discipline to control.

I will never forget my prior situation, and I want to help others with their financial struggles. Becoming debt free will not be easy, but my hope is that by reading (or referencing parts of this book), that you can get there faster.

A WORD ON DEBT PAYOFF AND MOTIVATION

"It is not the mountain we conquer, but ourselves."
–*Sir Edmund Hillary*
(Quote Investigator[1], 2016)

Many might not consider paying off debt to be the most exciting topic. But the trick is positive thinking, and turning negatives into positives – make it fun.

Human nature is to despise what we do not understand. This is true with virtually everything in life: misunderstandings lead to wars, damaged business or personal relationships, etc. Having a greater understanding of who, what, why, where, when, and how you got into debt and associated factors will serve as a good basis of escaping your situation. Do not be quick to blame others – be honest with yourself as you think about this.

Naturally positive people, or people that struggle with negativity gravitate towards positive thinking. While most of the time, this is of course preferred, this way of thinking puts less emphasis on improving things that need to be resolved. We see what we want to see, but need to meet reality and progress forward. This is especially true for those who may have problems with substance abuse as a means of forgetting issues – you can only escape reality temporarily this way, and cannot continue the downward spiral.

TERMINATE DEBT

Ask yourself why you want to be debt-free, and remind yourself of those reasons through your process. For many, that is to be able to afford a new home and build equity. Or perhaps you want to reduce overall stress, and not feel financially tied to a high-paying job, be able to relocate to another area (not underwater with your mortgage), etc.

You should also ask yourself: If you do not start paying off debt now, when will you? There is no better time than now.

Motivational objects (i.e. a paper weight with the message "Never give up", motivational posters, desktop backgrounds, etc.) can be helpful everyday reminders as well. Perhaps also print a photo of a dream home or vacation destination and frame it in an area of your house you spend a lot of time in.

Interestingly, hanging photos of things you do not like (to serve as a negative push/incentive) to achieve goals also helps.

Subscribing to reputable online newsletters can also help reinforce the message, with helpful tips and tricks.

Know that there is light at the end of the tunnel, and that your pursuit will become reality by looking at examples: drive by homes that you like, and aspire to move to. While of course, being careful to not move the target too far and aspire to move into large mansions – that defeats the goals of this book. While you may have the means later to move into a large house, for example, this might not last… whether that is due to a layoff and not being able to retain your same role in the same industry (income reduction), for health reasons, or other financial stress that may come later.

In the Tools and Processes section of this book, you will learn how to track debt payoff progress over time, and you can view progress in the form of a line graph.

Once you are debt-free, your opportunities are endless.

Do Not Get Discouraged

Do not be discouraged if your net worth today might not be where you want or need it to be. Once your debt is more easily managed, you can afford to invest more and diversify investments. At this stage, with more cash flow and an ability to invest, compounding interest will work in your favor, instead of the other way around with debt payments containing interest paid to lenders.

Keep in mind that the analogy of ups and downs from the stock market generally aligns well with one's wealth over the course of your lifetime. As long as you trend upward and maintain a forward trajectory, your goals have a better chance of materializing. At that point, you have momentum, which is a key point in debt payoff. It is similar to the analogy of a plane taking off of a runway – gravity pulls you down, but if you keep driving forward, faster, and keep the eye on the target, you will become airborne. Another good analogy that I like is climbing a mountain – you may be exhausted at certain points, especially with limited to no experience hiking and may think about giving up and returning. But you should think about how far you have come, why you set out on the journey (i.e. to lose weight, mental wellness seeing nature, etc.) and how much you will regret not finishing the journey.

Consider, too, that one does not need to have high income to pay off debt and live or retire well. There are plenty of cases where minimum or lower-wage earners have lived largely debt-free while living comfortably. The initial stage is the most difficult – diligence and self-discipline is key to pay debt off, which in turn builds confidence and more interest in paying off debt. High income earners such as movie stars and sports professionals have been known to go broke after buying expensive mansions, fancy cars, yachts, etc.

TERMINATE DEBT

A well-known Chinese proverb states: "The best time to plant a tree was 20 years ago. The second best time is now." (Caporicci, 2020). Translated for the context of this book, this means that while one's current finances would be better off if you started paying off debt and making investments in the past, there is no better time than now to start and make improvements. Even if you feel that you have hit 'rock bottom' and are considering bankruptcy as a final resort, there are always ways around difficult situations. The famous magician, Harry Houdini for example always challenged himself by placing himself in difficult situations, and took pride in finding a way out – you can too.

Debt payoff is not only about learning strategies and being dedicated to the zero-debt goal, but a true 360-degree approach also involves maintaining good physical and mental health. Talk to your primary care physician for advice, but exercising instead of a sedentary lifestyle has significant health benefits, as does healthy living. Avoid junk food, eat more natural foods, and keep an eye on calorie intake. It is important to maintain happiness, and the desire to live better. It also helps you be more productive, which can lead to higher pay at work, whether you work for someone else, or as a consultant for various clients. You might also want to consider a 'less is more' concept with your home – smaller home with a minimalist approach to decorating and amount of furnishings. Marie Kondo is a well-known author in this space if you are interested in reading more about that.

Many people have been able to achieve financial freedom, but do not necessarily flaunt their wealth by living in large homes, driving luxury cars, wearing gold watches, etc. In fact, most choose to hide their wealth to avoid attracting attention. If they are known to be wealthy, others may start to ask them for money which is frustrating, and puts them in an awkward position because they may never see the money again, and they will likely be asked again. It also attracts 'fake' people who are only interested in people with money. Even on the job, you may be unlikely to receive optimal salary increases or bonuses at the same rate/percentage as other high performers if your boss/company feels that you are already well-off. It is not unheard of for your own neighbors to be well-off, even to have a million-dollar plus net worth (a good book on this subject is *The Millionaire Next Door: The Surprising Secrets of America's Wealthy* by Thomas J. Stanley and William D. Danko.)

In the end, after debt is paid off (and you feel confident that you can maintain that trend), financial wealth has less value (as long as you have a decent savings buffer). Many older people do not define wealth in monetary terms, but in health terms: wealth = health.

DEBT-FREE EQUALS MORE SAVINGS EQUALS MORE FREEDOM

The more you save, the more financial security and personal freedom you have. But do not go overboard saving money, if that detracts from you being able to enjoy life and take occasional vacations to get off the grid and explore new areas and cultural experiences.

In business, a common strategy is to always plan for the worst, and hope for the best. You can follow the same approach in how you live and save for the future. If you save for at least 6 months worth of what you typically spend money on, with a bit of buffer, that should be sufficient. This allows you to live off this money in the event that you are laid off from work, until you find a new job.

If you had a problem with debt before and built a large savings pool over time, it may be tempting to spend money (i.e. frivolous purchases, etc.) This tends to have addictive/repeating qualities and should be avoided. More information on how this can be avoided can be found in the Eliminating Debt Triggers section of the book. Remember that with great power (or resources) comes great responsibility (Quote Investigator[2], 2015).

On the other hand, if you have a decent amount saved, you can still quickly deplete savings if you run into issues (i.e. layoff, health, other emergencies). You will start to 'feel the pain' as savings drop closer to zero and won't know what to do next. This is another important reason to subscribe to the 360-degree concept of becoming and remaining debt-free – owning and operating a business (preferably while diversifying in various areas) will help you maintain a healthy (more confident and long-lasting) savings pool.

BECOMING DEBT FREE DOES NOT MEAN YOU ARE DONE

"Just because you can't see something doesn't mean it isn't there. It's just waiting for the right time to show itself." –*Emma Hart* (Goodreads[2], n.d.)

Becoming debt-free is certainly something that you should celebrate and be proud of. But in no way should you hang a mental 'Mission Complete' banner and think your job is done.

Unexpected turns happen in life, and we all experience a mix of good and bad.

If too much time passes from when you pay off debt and you do not practice debt-management strategies during that time, you may forget how to best approach issues. This can lead you on the path back to debt.

By using the spreadsheet in the Tools and Processes section of this book, you will, by the nature of regularly updating the spreadsheet, reinforce the basic concepts and have a better picture of your financial situation.

ABOUT THE BOOK

Coincidentally, this book was published around the time of the annual winter solstice – the darkest and shortest day of the year. As with any struggle, even in the darkest of times, things will only get better. But, naturally, there will be some unexpected times of gloom, and darker days always emerge. By being prepared, you can help reduce or eliminate unexpected impacts.

The aim of this book is to:

- Identify debt triggers, and to help reduce or eliminate existing or potential influences. For example, how to effectively ignore consumerism, leverage your support network, improve overall health, and make small changes to how you think in general.

- Identify potential cost savings.

- Identify potential investment opportunities to create passive income.

- Assist with active or passive job searches (preferably, while you are still employed).

- Optimize your overall value/reputation at your existing job (i.e. having an intrapreneur/'ideas person' mentality, becoming a subject-matter expert in various areas, etc.)

- Provide entrepreneurial guidance to help you create redundant (multiple) external income sources for financial security.

- Introduce new tools and procedures to help you create and manage a budget, and other financial interests.

The primary focus of this book is controlling bad debt to then focus on net worth. It is important to emphasize that not all debt is bad. 'Good' and 'bad' debt is situational, and depends on one's lifestyle. For example, owning a home and paying a mortgage may make sense for one person (good debt), but not another (ultimately being bad debt). References to debt in this book refer to bad debt, unless otherwise stated.

In some cases, material may seem repetitive. That is by design (albeit written differently) to help reinforce concepts, and also because there is cross-over between debt target areas. It is also helpful to highlight concepts where appropriate for those who do not feel that they need to read the whole book, but want to reference specific areas for help.

This book is designed to be informational, but not a single point of reference. For one, while I have experience managing my personal debts, I do not know of specific unique challenges and trials of others, and thus I do not have all the answers. More importantly, I am not a financial advisor, tax professional, attorney, psychologist, therapist, or other medical professional. You may want to consider expanding your support network to optimize your financial decision making. Further, although the advice in this book will likely help many, results are not guaranteed – this is the starting point, and you must do your homework and build/reinforce your support network to help you along your path.

Always remember – *you want* to be debt-free. Push hard to make it happen. With less debt and burden, you have more control over your future.

ELIMINATING DEBT TRIGGERS

"Don't become part of someone else's cause or crusade. Pursue your
own self interest. Always."
(The X-Files Transcripts Archive[2], n.d.)

I shared this quote because I felt it was one of the best ones I have seen
that could be applied to peer pressure (i.e. 'keeping up with the
Joneses') or marketing/commercial pressure to spend money. Or
perhaps pressure to drive a fancy car to show that you 'made it'. You
should not be embarrassed to drive a basic sedan for example, even if
it is used and 10+ years old. It is after all your life.

The quote also supports maintaining 'stubborn' personalities to not
spend money or make contributions to certain charities, workplace or
religious collections, etc., if you simply choose not to, or are not in a
true financial position to do so. You may not be liked or you may suffer
other repercussions as a result, but if someone does not like you
because you chose not to spend money on certain occasions (and do
not participate in events supported by collections), there should be no
'ill' feelings, questions, or repercussions. If you do suffer from any of
that, you may need to reconsider your friendships and associations.

Debt triggers involve a multitude of factors, however, and this section
will review the most common ones.

LACK OF A SAVINGS OR EMERGENCY ACCOUNT

Having a savings account is critical to work around issues that impact
your financial well-being.

You should at least have 3 months of savings to pay for bills and day-to-day expenses if you lost a job, and preferably 6 months for greater protection. Of course, if you have more than that, the better off you will be, and the more confidence you will have, including feeling more at ease when situations arise.

If you do not have a savings account and run into issues, help is always available. You can usually get help with fundamentals such as food, clothing, and shelter. Your town office or city hall can help point you in the right direction if needed.

General Health and Wellness

No Longer Able to Address General Home Maintenance

If, for example, you purchased a new home on the basis (with a budgeting implication) that you would be able to fix issues and perform renovations yourself, mow your own lawn, clear snow, rake leaves, and handle general landscape work yourself, you would naturally experience challenges if you have new health issues.

In this case, community programs exist where volunteers can perform tasks such as mowing your lawn. If this is needed, call your town's office or city hall and ask for more information. You can also join your town/city's community group on Facebook and ask there.

If you need to sell your home, many newly licensed real estate agents can potentially negotiate a low (or no) commission deal to sell your house in exchange for putting in a good word for them with your friends and family to help them build a customer base.

Sudden Health Issues

If something unexpected happens with a big impact, such as the need to have major surgery, cancer treatment, etc., and you cannot afford the payments (i.e. no insurance, or lack of coverage for a specific treatment), you can ask for help instead of going thousands of dollars in debt. Various websites such as GoFundMe are built for this purpose. You can create an ad to share your situation, provide evidence (if you believe that will help), and ask for donations. This helps go around the awkward situation of needing to ask friends and family for help, and you can earn new friends in the process and return their favor later as a courtesy (to support the 'pay it forward' concept). The latter is generally not required, nor is reimbursement.

MENTAL TRIGGERS

The mind is very powerful. Learning to control the way you think (the cause), being prepared for worst-case scenarios, and not being vulnerable to various situations can be valuable assets when dealing with debt (the effect).

AVOID BEING UNDER THE INFLUENCE

Drugs do not address the source of problems, they just cover them. It is easy to ignore and prolong issues with any form of drugs.

Some people may not consider alcoholic and caffeinated beverages to be drugs, but they are – they alter behavior. Alcohol is used by some to de-stress, and caffeine to focus and stay alert.

Even with an occasional one or two alcoholic drinks, self restraint and self-discipline are not optimal. It is therefore easier for someone in this situation to be more apt to purchase one or more things that they may not normally purchase, or purchase something that they were hesitant to buy before when they were more aware of their financial situation. The same can be said with caffeine.

Review cancellation policies if the order has not yet shipped, or return policies if the package is on its way. It may be possible to refuse a package if unopened with no return shipping charges required. It depends on the situation. You may be responsible for restocking fees, however.

To avoid debt triggers under the influence, keep your wallet far away (if you are in your own home), or even better – avoid drugs/alcohol altogether.

ANXIETY AND DEPRESSION

Anxiety and depression can be genetic, or it may be triggered by the loss of a loved one (friends, family, or even a pet).

You may try to fill an emotional gap with unnecessary bulk buying/mass purchases, and frivolous spending. If this becomes a problem (this can lead to a hoarding situation), cancel your credit cards, get into a debt repayment plan, and only use a debit card linked with a checking account. This way you know that you are only spending money that you have.

Anxiety and depression have also been known to be an underlying cause of overeating, including eating junk food – all of which can lead to more health issues such as diabetes, etc. Overeating can also drain the wallet. As an aside, junk food may be cheap, but ultimately cost you more in health expenses and lost opportunities as your energy level drops, and self-image declines.

If you struggle with anxiety or depression, you may find speaking with a therapist or psychologist helpful. Local community groups may also exist, in addition to online forums.

GAMBLING

Gambling is a multi-billion dollar industry. It is never a charity, and gambling organizations do not take winning well (except to advertise winnings, to attract more business). Losses translate to more challenging games with higher odds. Some gambling organizations have also been known to compliment winning streaks with free meals and nights to pull the attention away from game tables.

The odds of any game – a scratch ticket, or a million-dollar drawing – are always stacked against you. You are unlikely to win, and when you do, it is unlikely to be any significant amount. Small winnings only encourage more spending, and you are likely to lose those winnings with more purchases. Gas station clerks, for example, are notorious for asking if you want to use winnings to buy more tickets, and you have to learn to say no. Do not make gambling a habit as well – if needed, do not carry cash and you will be less apt to spend it on scratch tickets and drawings. Luckily, many states do not allow one to play the lottery with credit card funds to help people that have a gambling addiction. If you have gambled online, remove your funding source and/or set gambling limits.

Big winnings have historically also attracted unwanted attention – i.e. homes getting robbed, death threats, and general bad luck. It ruins families and lives. Winning the lottery is not something you want to aspire to, especially if you cannot claim anonymously. There are lots of jealous people out there, and they will try to get a piece of the pie, even if they do not know you. The amount of pressure will be high, and some may also scam you (i.e. asking for money for a supposed charity, and taking it as their own... or worse yet, the charity misspending funds knowing the source was from lottery winnings). Jobs can be at risk, etc. Be careful what you wish for.

It is always best if you can earn money on your own, gradually increasing wealth, versus winning a large amount of money from the lottery. You will appreciate it more, and learn to spend it wisely as money accumulates.

If you have a gambling problem, you can call your state's gambling addiction hotline. Local community groups may also exist, in addition to online forums where you can be anonymous (just beware of 'trolls' who have nothing better to do than ridicule people in comments – ignore them).

IMPULSE BUYING

When shopping online, a one to three step buying process makes it very easy to order. This is more convenient, but is naturally more likely to encourage spending, leading to issues.

Luckily, many online retailers do not immediately fulfill orders, and the order may be cancellable within a 30-60 minute window, or more. Check the cancellation policy. If you change your mind, and you are within the cancellation window, there is likely to be no charge, a temporary charge that will go away after a period of time, or your charge will be automatically refunded. If you need to cancel right away, and there is not a way for you to do this by yourself, instead of emailing customer support, call customer support or use live chat for faster response.

The best way to avoid impulse buying is to resist the temptation to buy. Wait the purchase out by perhaps a week, to think about it. It may go away, which is more disappointing if it is a unique item, but assuming it is a want and not a need, there is no true loss. It is just another 'thing' that you do not need in the house. If needed, go for a walk or find something else to do. Take comfort in knowing that if you ever needed to sell it, it would likely be a tough sell and you may not be able to recover what you spent fully.

FRIVOLOUS PURCHASES

"We are living in a material world" –*Madonna*
(Lyrics, n.d.)

The media constantly glorifies abundance, wealth, and things – after all, this is what many aspire to, as part of the American dream – and thus portrayals of (i.e. movies) and offering byproducts of the dream (i.e. fancy jewelry, ornate antiques) sell well. But, the American dream is a moving target, with no guaranteed lasting effect, and is also an overinflated (and overrated) reality. You would not want to really live the dream of one or more large houses, a yacht, fast cars, etc. Remember: what you have at any given moment can easily be taken away. There can be legal challenges that drain your bank account for those who go after your successes, and countless other reasons.

Remember too: the bigger the house, the fancier the car, the more stuff you have that you do not need, the harder it is to sell if you are no longer capable to make payments or otherwise afford the lifestyle. Things change all the time. On the latter, Heraclitus, an ancient philosopher from Greece, is known to have said: "change is the only constant in life" (PsychCentral, 2017).

It is okay to gift yourself with small inexpensive purchases every so often, and this is actually encouraged. If you hold back too much without spending money on occasional indulgences, you may be more likely to spend your money on one-off expensive purchases which should be avoided.

Avoid Buying Large Homes

No matter how big, or how extravagant your house is, someone else has more/bigger. And your neighbors will likely try to outdo your efforts.

This may also seem repetitive, but for a significant investment such as a home, always remember that you may have means today to afford and maintain the property, but you can never be sure about the near or distant future.

If you have toured large historic mansions such as the ones in Newport, Rhode Island, you have seen some of the best examples of excess and over-spending that was primarily done to show off. There was a time where these large portrayals of success helped prolong a wealthy family's political influence and power, but these homes were otherwise purely for 'show'. Future generations found it increasingly more difficult to maintain the homes, and some highly customized and elaborate homes were difficult to sell. Ownership of many large historic homes was ultimately transferred to preservation and conservation organizations where there is heavy reliance on donations, special events, weddings, and large numbers of tourists to maintain them. For other homes, they have fallen to ruin, and many have since been demolished.

Only billionaires or multi-millionaires with a reliable source of continuous revenue can afford similar homes today, and interestingly, the size of homes tends to increase for people in this category to show off. But the same trend continues with issues of ongoing maintenance in the future, and sadly, without historical value, many may be torn down – especially custom homes that do not have mass appeal.

You don't want a ruin to be your family legacy, and you also do not want to make it difficult for future generations to maintain your home when family financial resources start to fade, unless there is a very good investment strategy to retain and enhance (for inflation) available maintenance funds.

You should also consider whether selling a large home in the area is an easy sale if you ever need (or want) to sell quickly. For example, if you find a job in a different part of the country and do not have an option to work remotely, or you absorb a significant pay cut.

As an aside, when buying homes, it is generally worth it in the long-term (i.e. 6+ years). But it may be worth renting if you want to stay somewhere short-term (i.e. 1-5 years).

AVOID BUYING FRIVOLOUS OBJECTS

As a 'commoner' touring/visiting historic mansions, people may be tempted to buy things that remind them of what they have seen in the homes simply because they like them, or as something to aspire to. Some people may make this a habit, similar to what is sometimes known as the 'antique bug', where someone grows a collection of valuable antiques. Or, they may buy very expensive jewelry, or objects for display. While all of these look nice, and would be good 'conversation pieces', these kinds of purchases should be controlled: too much excess is bad for the wallet, and your well-being. Equally important: jewelry and display case objects tend to depreciate significantly. Antiques also do not appeal to everyone, and similar to collectables, you will likely have a difficult time selling, and the amount of time listing/relisting and dealing with queries about items for sale may not be worth the trouble in the end, when/if you choose to sell. You should also avoid buying things to impress others – it can backfire and work against you if others think you are well-off.

Keep in mind that the more elaborate an object is, or the more customized it is, the harder it typically is to sell it. For example, gothic revival furniture with elaborate carved woodwork has a small audience and cannot be easily sold on the open market. When buying to resell later, it is often best to buy something that has mass appeal with neutral colors. But it is also important to buy something because you like it. You have to strike a balance between the two.

The more things you have, the more time it would take to sell everything. If you chose a quick sell path (if you are lucky to have a sponsor), such as with an estate sale or auction, expect big fees, and people generally expect to pay less for things at these events (unless something is truly rare or scarce), versus selling everything independently on the private market (i.e. Facebook Marketplace, eBay, Craigslist).

The job of marketing professionals is to convince you that you need something that is not necessarily needed. You should also avoid watching infomercials, and submitting to superficial advertising.

Avoid becoming a hoarder - frivolous buying sprees are often triggered by the loss of a loved one, job loss, divorce, short or long-term illness including depression and anxiety, or other hardships. If you are on a negative track, search for "hoarder estate sale" on EstateSales.org or EstateSales.net and look at the photos – you do not want to end up like them, and the photos they take are usually in the best light (it looks worse in person).

A brief anecdote: I read an article written by a former homeowner. He invested in a historic home and collected the finest period antiques to furnish his home, complete with rare first-edition books. Sadly, everything went up in flames and he lost everything. While fires are rare, you should keep this in mind when you buy too many things, especially expensive things. Insurance protection is also very expensive if you were to get everything appraised and insured. The loss of historic items in a private residence is also a shame, and these items are best kept in museums for more people to enjoy.

Finally, buying frivolous items is not limited to the home. It is important to stress that this could mean buying jewelry, coins or other items that are not always visible and stashed away. It can also extend to fancy suitcases, briefcases, purses, backpacks, etc.

If you are a parent, you should not be pressured to buy the best for your kids to align your kid with peers, or even to 'outdo' other kids to show off your family's wealth, or try to make your child popular. There is value in doing the complete opposite, especially for the goals of this book. You want to propagate long-term financial wellness and be a model example. This includes explaining to your child that it is not always best to be popular, that popularity is short-lived, and that people who are overly attracted to expensive things or well off people are fake and not worth associating with.

AVOID FANCY CARS

Cars look great in the showroom and in marketing materials/videos. But once you sign the paperwork, get the keys, and drive off the dealer's lot, it is no longer a perfect car. The car immediately depreciates in value. And you will start to notice dings and scratches – it always seems that new cars are magnets for people to walk past with pocket zippers scratching the metal, and open their car doors to bang against. Beyond that, insurance and car registration costs are highest when the car is new. Insurance costs also skyrocket for fast sports cars, as statistics suggest a higher risk for the insurance company.

Once you deviate from well-known, common car models, you may also run into more problems. For example, a Honda Civic has a good reputation with a good reliability track record which makes it an economical solution for the masses. But other mid-tier luxury brands may require you to bring the vehicle into the garage more often for repairs. Repair costs tend to also be cheaper for common car models, as the parts are readily available, and they do not always require special training to install. A high-end car with a special engine, for example, would likely cost much more to repair.

Consumer Reports and other independent research companies that do not accept advertising dollars from the subject areas they review are good sources to confirm reliability. Kelly Blue Book (KBB) will help you determine current resale value for your area.

It is always better to buy used as well, as long as the vehicle repair history checks out okay (you may want to order a CarFax report).

From a psychological perspective, if you own a fancy/expensive car and drive it regularly, it places you in a different world and mindset that can put you at greater risk of spending more to keep up with others you associate with (who are likely to also be successful).

There are many successful people out there that are still driving 10+ year old cars that are standard, base model sedans. Their friends, family, and coworkers do not treat them any differently. These people have the current means to buy a more expensive luxury car, but they chose not to... perhaps considering the depreciation and return of investment at the end of the car's life.

As an aside, when buying cars, you should weigh buying new, leasing new, or buying used. There are pros and cons of all. When you buy new, you have a longer-term commitment, but generally a worry-free ownership where major repairs may not be required for many years. When you lease, you may get stuck paying for mileage overage if you take many day trips or long-distance vacations. And when you buy used, you pay less up front, but may end up paying for large unexpected repair bills, and have to deal with more frequent car replacements due to the limited lifespan of the car and it already having at least one prior owner.

If you trade in your old car, make sure that you get fair market value for it, in addition to the best price for the new car purchase. These are two separate transactions.

DEPRECIATION

Virtually anytime you buy something new, it will depreciate. The reason is because it (or a similar derivative) can be, or has been known to be, bought elsewhere cheaper once alternate ownership has been assumed.

Cars are the most commonly cited example of depreciation, but this applies to any new retail item. For example, yard sales or eBay feature items at significant discounts even if it is not that old. Home values can also depreciate in certain markets or economic conditions.

Buying used is generally the best way to save money, and auctions, estate sales, yard sales, and private online sales are great ways to achieve this. You will need to weigh safety risks associated with where or how certain items were used, if someone is reputable, etc., but the same can be said about buying new as well (maybe something can still legally be sold as new if it was a return, and mileage or ownership was under a certain threshold/return window).

PROTECT OTHERS

Debt can be caused if someone in your family takes ownership of your property after you pass away, and such property has encumbrances to resolve, or needs to be repaired before they can move in or sell the property.

If someone needs to resolve an estate with extensive items bound to it, life insurance is a great way to complement the process since it provides a cash source to draw from as needed to assist. If for some reason you do not qualify for life insurance (in other words, rejected after applying), there are slightly higher-cost insurance plans available. Or, you can wait 7 years until your application history clears from national life insurance databases, such as the one MIB maintains, and apply again with a clean slate, hoping for cheaper life insurance. Most life insurance companies only require you to answer questions up to 5 years back.

You should also be careful with how you invest your money. It should preferably be invested in accounts that can be easily accessible. If it is an offshore account, especially one subject to various regulations that might not support inheritance, it will cause difficulties for your family. Likewise, if you invest large sums of money in Bitcoin or other digital currency, your family should know how they can convert that to cash if necessary. Avoid storing digital currency in highly secure offline storage with fingerprint access, or unknown passwords/pins, as this cannot be redeemed to support your estate after you pass away.

Some families have a primary checking or savings account that has multiple family members on it, or at least the executor. When an estate needs to be resolved, it makes the process much smoother this way.

AVOID SCAMS AND IDENTITY THEFT

"Trust no one."
(The X-Files Transcripts Archive[1], n.d.)

Falling victim to scams and identity theft is another quick way to fall into debt. You cannot stop criminals from being criminal, but you can make it difficult for them to choose you as a victim, or take precautions to lessen the impact to yourself if you do become a victim.

Scams do not always involve people trying to rip you off by taking your payment and then not shipping something. They may send you something, but the product may be counterfeit, inferior quality, or otherwise not as represented. If for example you ordered two products, and received one, or you were offered a promotion and you did not receive discounts or other special offers, it may have been a simple mistake, but it could also very well be a scam.

These strategies can help you:

- Check site reviews. Sometimes these can be fabricated (completely made-up). Or sometimes they can be a result of actual customers, but the customers were reimbursed by the publisher, seller, or manufacturer in exchange for a 4 or 5 star review. If too many 5 star reviews are seen in a specific period of time, consider that suspicious. Check reviews on other sites for a fair comparison. Use the product code to search online against (this is different from a vendor's store code at times, which is intentionally more visible to deter these kinds of searches, mainly for price comparison/anti-competition).

- Remember the old advice: if it is too good to be true, it probably is. This is almost always true. If for example you see an original painting from a famous painter for less money, it may not be actually produced by the artist. It may be a reproduction, print, or giclée/embellishment (still nice, but less collector quality). It is possible that it could be real, but many times a lack of provenance (tie/proof from the line of succession/ownership from the artist) will remove value. Damage and restoration can also have an impact on value.

- Use secure sites (look for the lock icon in the browser address bar).

- Use antivirus/malware/endpoint protection software, preferably with VPN to mask your location and activity. Bitdefender is a good program, as are many others such as Kaspersky, McAfee, and Norton products.

- Do not write down passwords. Use an encrypted password storage service such as LastPass, or the one bundled with your antivirus/malware/endpoint protection software. Log out when there is no need to use this, and log in only when needed for extra precaution.

- Be careful/protective with sharing your social security number, photo, and driver's license. Especially on less common digital currency trading sites, which hackers target for easy access to this information.

- Check the seller's reputation on third party sites. The Better Business Bureau (BBB) is a good resource, but people can supposedly pay for higher ratings as well. The reviews are what matter. Consumer Reports is a good resource, as are Google reviews, and industry-specific review sites (i.e. Angie's List for contractors).

- Buy a paper shredder and shred your confidential documents at home. Do not bring them in to drop-off locations, as these are targets for criminals, and the documents may not get picked up by third party shredders until much later.

- When it is time to sell or exchange your computer, always perform a secure erase on the drive with at least three full passes (Department of Defense method is suitable). Remove your hard drive and contact a data destruction service such as Shred-It. These companies typically work with businesses and they may push back a bit as a result, but they DO work with residential customers as well. There just may be a bit of a wait until a truck can make it to your location. These services are very good as they can provide you with a list of serial numbers for all drives which serves as proof that your drives were destroyed, and transfers liability to the company. My only suggestion with this is to note and print serial numbers from the hard drives to give to the tech when they arrive, and compare the list they present to you from their scanner before you sign. Sometimes they make up their own serial number prefix and shorten a long serial number, and it can be a hassle to get this corrected after the fact through an amendment.

Never include a hard drive with a computer, regardless of pressure from a buyer to include it (even with buyer threats of backing away from a deal). Of course mention that the hard drive is not included in your listing.

- Hire a media shredding service (preferably on-site) to destroy old media such as CDs, disks, and USB drives. They may also be able to shred old phones. This shredding may need to be done separately from hard drive shredding for environmental purposes, but it can be done. Always push for on-site shredding, as you cannot trust the diligence of others with your security.

- When products arrive, always open the packages and ensure that they are authentic/genuine parts. It is not uncommon to receive counterfeit products from multi-vendor sites. For example, I received counterfeit landscape string trimmer replacements, as well as counterfeit shaving blades, which were both safety hazards if they were used. Sometimes spending more money to get products directly from the manufacturer is worth it for peace of mind.

In general, always be on guard, even with people who come across as very nice people. Never trust someone who initially asks you to trust them. Trust is always earned, and then you should still be on guard. As Ronald Reagan once said, "trust, but verify" (Ronald Reagan Presidential Library & Museum, 1987). The time you spend in taking precautions and proactive measures is considerably lower than the time spent repairing a credit history or otherwise dealing with scammers and other criminals.

PERSONA

Maintaining a certain persona is key when trying to pay off debt fast. These strategies may help:

- Try to assume and project a positive attitude and way of thinking. But at the same time, as stated earlier, be realistic and not 'too' positive in a way that you blow off your debt issues – they need to be addressed, preferably sooner rather than later. If you assume and project a positive attitude, other successful people will gravitate toward you, and they can connect you with other successful people and new opportunities. These people can also serve as your support network. If it helps, place objects in your work area and throughout your home (especially where you frequent most) that make you happy – this can be a knick-knack, something that a close friend gave you, etc.

- Similarly, remove bad influences. Do not associate with people who complain all the time, especially those who back-stab others. They probably do the same to you to please others since they feed off negativity.

- Do not live an extravagant lifestyle, including buying 'showy' or frivolous purchases – there is no logic in attempting to compete with or outdo others. There will always be someone with more money, a bigger house, more expensive car, more things, etc. Doing so will push the good people away, and attract the bad (who are interested in your money and access to free stuff). These people will also quickly disappear if you lose everything. Example: research the life of Madame Sherri (Society for the Protection of New Hampshire Forests, n.d.)

- Catch on to hoarding tendencies early. Lots of materialistic objects, or even everyday items such as paper and mail piling up, can contribute to stress. Scan papers with text recognition enabled for easy retrieval, and to clear clutter and shred. You can also sell unused or unnecessary items. If you do perform spring cleaning, be aware of environmental disposal requirements when cleaning – consider dropping chemicals off to local household hazardous collection events, taking unused drugs to drug 'take back' events, disposing of sharps to sharp collection boxes typically at hospitals.

- Resistance is key – if you want to buy something, wait. If you must, put it on hold, or on a wish list. Think about it for at least a week while keeping your debt reduction goals in mind. Sure, it is possible that the item may no longer be available at a certain point, but that is probably for the best. Do not fall into the trap of buying to try to resell (generally speaking, it is unlikely that you will profit, considering marketing and your time).

- Stand your ground and don't allow yourself to be pressured by others. Others may not like this, but you must remember that this is your life, and your interests – not theirs. Do what is best for you.

AVOID BORROWING

- Do not ask friends and family for money. Go to the bank for loans if needed, but borrow wisely. Know your monthly payment, and especially be aware of fluctuating payments if the rate is variable.

- It is best to always borrow with a fixed rate, even if it is slightly higher. This gives you greater peace of mind.

- With commercialism, and ease of buying, many people buy or lease brand new cars (for example) not out of necessity, but to keep up with others they know who do the same and to give an impression of being successful or not cheap. Do not let this be you! You will not like feeling stuck with a high monthly payment for multiple years, and the stress that comes with it.

- If you need money, you can also try raising money online. Many crowd-sourced sites are catered specifically for people that run into emergencies, and people have been successful raising money there. Just remember to be truthful, and honest with yourself – use this as a last resort. You will typically need to identify yourself and your name may get indexed by search engines, meaning current or future employers could potentially see this and make decisions (right or wrong) based on the ad content and situation.

CHOOSE WISELY TO AVOID LOSING MONEY

"But choose wisely, for while the true Grail will bring you life, the false Grail will take it from you." –*Spoken by the fictional Grail Knight character in the movie "Indiana Jones and the Last Crusade."* (IMDB, n.d.)

Many vendors charge very high consulting fees, or other fees that are way over market price.

You should always get more than one quote from multiple vendors (preferably, at least three).

Vendor selection is not about finding the cheapest, but the middle ground while considering the vendor's reputation, and also factoring in your gut feeling when speaking with them. Cheaper contractors may cut corners, or may not have been fully transparent with you and start asking for more money to finish the job or charging 'surprise' fees that were not discussed initially. The challenge sometimes is that many vendors will not (or cannot) provide an accurate quote before a job starts due to unknown factors, but there are plenty of companies that do not disclose things up front knowing that they may be turned away if the homeowner knows the true cost.

Avoid resellers or middlemen when possible to avoid unnecessary markups.

You should also avoid hiring friends, as you do not want to damage your relationship with them if they produce subpar work, or their schedule is unreliable with the timing of your project.

Keep in mind that some states do not require contractors to become licensed in certain professions. For example, a home handyman may not require being licensed, nor a landscaping professional.

Hiring specialists such as financial advisors can be very helpful, but they can also cost thousands of dollars which could have been put in investments (i.e. index funds) which have the benefit of compounding over time. The cost/benefit should be reviewed before making a decision and signing any contract. Some investment fund companies offer free or low-cost access to financial advisors, depending on your assets. If you are not financially savvy, you could benefit from follow-ups, encouragement, and motivation from a real person and pursuing help from a financial advisor could very well be worth it to keep you on track with your goals.

CREDIT CARDS AND PROMOTIONAL OFFERS

You should be very careful about credit cards.

People new to credit cards tend to have good intentions to be responsible. But external factors can get in the way, and you may intend to borrow just a few hundred dollars and pay it back soon. But that does not always happen, and things can quickly escalate from there with payments getting out of control.

You should be wary of offers such as:

- Introductory low (or 0%) credit promotional rates. The periods offered may seem long, but time quickly passes, and then you are stuck paying a much higher rate with a potentially large balance.

- No payments for 'x' amount of time. It may seem like you get something for free, but then reality sinks in when you have payments.

- Balance transfer offers. This fixes a symptom of high payment for a quick fix/temporary relief, but does not address the root source of high balances. Rates increase after a certain period of time. You also do not want to make a habit/common practice of transferring balances as this activity is noted and maintained on your credit report. Too many new credit cards or cards with limited history/ownership does not impact your credit score well.

Compounding interest rates on high credit card balances hurts, and becomes an ongoing cycle that perpetuates one's negative or low net worth.

Credit cards are good for convenience, if you can pay balances off quickly, preferably every month to avoid interest payments. Credit cards are also good for buyer protection and to have on hand for emergencies.

If your credit card spending gets out of hand, consider shredding them (if plastic). Or if you have a metal credit card, you can call the credit card company and ask them to send you a postage paid return envelope where you can send it back, and they will destroy it for you (metal credit cards cannot be shredded in home shredders).

Debit cards with a Visa or Mastercard logo can be a good alternative to credit cards, because it forces you to spend only what you have in your checking account.

Be careful about saving your credit card information with vendors online. If you placed an order with them before, hackers can gain access to your account and place orders. Since you already have an existing relationship with the vendor, it can be difficult for credit card companies sometimes to support a dispute claim as a result. A hacker once gained control of an account I owned on an ecommerce site and used my credit card information to place an order. Luckily, I was able to stop the order in time.

Urgency and Sales Pressure

- Door-to-door sales agents are masters in creating urgency and sales pressure. Although they come across as nice people, they are not your friend. The only way they may remember you in the future is if they enter your information in a Customer Relationship Management (CRM) system to act like they know and remember you if you placed an order before and call in/email (or they contact you).

- Mobile device push alerts/notifications and emails cause urgency by design. The best notifications make you feel guilty when an item you 'watched' or 'liked' is no longer available/sold to encourage faster shopping next time. Push alerts are common with applications such as eBay, Groupon, LivingSocial, and Facebook Marketplace. They can also be used to let you know when an auction listing (for example) is ending as a 'last chance' offer, or for sellers to send you special offers/discounts if they noticed that you saved/liked their listing. To avoid these aggressive alerts, you can uninstall the applications, and disable push notifications. You should be careful about automatic application updates as these sometimes add new alert features or overlook/reset existing settings.

- Email marketing, cold calls, snail mail, and TV or online advertising are other ways to create urgency (demand generation). Just remember you have your own priorities, and it is likely that you may be able to negotiate better deals on your own terms with the same companies when things are slower with them (or outside of their current promotions).

- Keep in mind that discounts and sales might be for less popular or overstock items as well, so you should be guarded about what you are buying.

- Marketers will emphasize a 'buy now, or else you may lose out' message. This can be true, especially for limited edition/release or overstock items, but remember that these items likely fall into the 'want' rather than the 'need' category.

- Those who are financially adept may joke that while a 75% or higher discount is good, not buying the item at all and saving the difference is even better. Similarly, you should know that some sellers are known to market 'x' percent off, while also increasing their prices to make it seem like a good deal. Always shop around to make sure you are getting the best price.

- Always ask about the condition of products, and never assume that they are damage free. Also ask about the life expectancy of the product, and whether it comes with a lifetime warranty.

- Even for offers of 'free' products or services, there is no such thing as free. There is always an expectation or understanding associated for a future return. Read the fine print, and ask what 'the catch' is with the deal.

EMAIL MARKETING (A.K.A. 'SPAM')

- If you remember subscribing to a newsletter or other form of email marketing, you can click on the unsubscribe link (usually at the bottom of the email).

- If you do not remember subscribing to a message, or giving permission for a vendor to share your email with partners, click on the 'report spam' button/link in your application to report abuse. This usually alerts the email service provider the person is using that they are not abiding by email marketing laws and policies. This will likely filter these messages out in the future without needing to unsubscribe. If you unsubscribe from these kinds of unsolicited emails, the sender will be able to confirm your email address and you may receive further spam from them/their associates.

- If you do not want to unsubscribe from emails, you can optionally reduce email frequency. Some vendors offer this option after you click on the unsubscribe link. For example, instead of daily messages, you can receive weekly emails.

- You can often unsubscribe from all of the company's emails as well. For example, if the company is a publisher with multiple online media brands, they may have an easy way to unsubscribe from all of the brands at once.

SOCIAL CIRCLES AND PEER PRESSURE

You should make wise choices with friends, associating with coworkers outside of work, and personal relationships.

As stated before, you will need to make difficult decisions to save money and pay off debt. If you are struggling financially or just trying to save money, you may need to learn how to say no to frequent restaurant invitations, for example, even at work (if the company does not pay for or reimburse for them). This may give people the wrong impression if you consistently say no to invitations, so it is okay to attend these events on occasion. You may need to ask to come along, if you were normally invited before, to reinforce that you have not 'checked out' but only choose to occasionally pass.

You should also avoid people who seem to only like you for your money, if you are generally well-off (but have a lot of debt).

If you are asked for money/donations at work, or on social media, it is okay to not contribute if you are not in a position to do so. If someone later asks you individually (applying pressure), say you will think about it. They will be unlikely to ask again.

The same concept applies to retail stores or restaurants asking if you want to donate money. It is okay to say "not today, thanks".

Also, do not feel like you have to follow others, especially successful people in your family/social circle. You do not need to have a child, you do not need to buy a house, and you do not need a new car. Caring for a small pet, living in an apartment, and owning a 5 or 10+ year old car is just fine.

IDENTIFY COST SAVINGS: HOW YOU CAN SAVE MONEY

It is important to have a healthy savings account, including a buffer in your checking account to prepare for unknowns and emergencies. You should never be in a position, for example, to have to decline simple things that others take for granted: going to an annual physical, the dentist, a close friend or family member's birthday party, etc. These are examples of things for which you should draw from your checking account (budgeted items), and alternatively, a savings account allows you to temporarily draw money for unbudgeted/unknown events.

You do not need to sacrifice everything. The idea is to stop being frivolous and making unnecessary purchases. Sell excess. You can still buy small or inexpensive things every so often (which in fact is encouraged, to prevent splurging or binge buying), but if habits get out of hand, you need to practice self-discipline to deviate from such habits.

As stated before, at least 6 months of savings to support yourself and your family is generally recommended, but having more in savings of course helps for large emergencies beyond temporary issues such as layoffs.

When it comes to savings, remember that you will save more by not buying something at all, rather than buying just to save 'x' percent.

Some common savings techniques include bringing lunch into work instead of buying it at the cafeteria, turning lights off at home when they are not being used, and turning the heat or air conditioning down when not home (including creating a heating/cooling schedule if your device home temperature control supports this). You should also consider reducing waste (for example, tearing half of a paper towel off of a whole sheet and using the other part later, using less paper towel sheets when cleaning, cutting new sponges in half to prolong the life, etc.)

Most debt reduction books might suggest that you stop buying coffee every day if you commute to work. You do not need to do that, but it certainly helps. It is an accumulation of small things saved that makes a big impact.

Other common savings strategies involve renting a guest room or unused room in a home for extra income. This generally appeals more to younger people versus older generations as they may have more valuables around and might not be comfortable with 'strangers' living in their home. If you do rent a room, make sure that you get the renter's permission to do a background check, including a criminal history review and credit review. Always collect a security deposit, regardless of any push-back you get from them. And always be fair with room rent based on the size of the room and utilities, so the person leasing the room from you knows they are getting a good deal/market rate and will likely stay longer as a result (equating to a longer revenue stream for you).

Subscribe and Save/Automatic Shipments

Subscribe and save, or automatic shipment features such as those offered by Amazon or Chewy are easy to set up and they can save you money, but you may find that this automated convenience makes it easy to forget that you have orders on their way. The services typically give you an advance notice at least a few days away to allow you to cancel or change your shipment, but these emails may arrive while you are on a call for work, etc., and can be forgotten.

What helps is if you take note of the precise times that you need orders, rather than arbitrarily setting timed delivery. That way these services work for you, by giving you less to worry about (not having to make sure something is always fully stocked, or if something is about to run out), and also saving you money.

If you do forget to cancel an order that is already on its way, many vendors will work with you to return it. You may have an option to refuse an order if it is unopened by bringing the package back to the shipping company's local customer service office. Or, the vendor's customer service team may be able to provide a prepaid shipping label to send it back. Do keep an eye out for 'last chance to change or cancel' emails, because having to return items is still a hassle.

RECYCLING AND REUSING: CREATIVE HACKS TO EXTEND YOUR DOLLAR

The list of ways you can save money by extending the life of items, or finding creative uses (or hacks) is endless. Some methods will require more of your time, and you will have to assess whether it is worth the extra effort to save. But this section is meant to show you another way to save some money, which as you know adds up in the 'big picture'. It is also meant to serve as a means to help you brainstorm money saving ideas in the context of recycling, reusing, and extending the life of products that apply to you.

A common 'hack' is cutting new sponges in half. This prolongs the life of a sponge, and also allows you to use one half for your dishes, and the other for pet dishes (for example).

Another 'hack' that some people do is create their own natural laundry detergent. This can save a considerable amount of money long-term, but you really need to know what you are doing to do this right. You do not want to use volatile/toxic chemicals, and you want to make sure that the detergent is safe for your laundry machine and also for your skin. You should also be aware of appropriate first-aid if a child gets access to this. The benefit of buying ready-made laundry detergent is that it typically clearly provides first-aid instructions, and lists all ingredients on the label for quick reference.

It may be worth searching for craft blogs or 'how to' articles for other ideas.

Another interesting idea is that if you live in an area where leaves need to be raked in the fall, or where snow falls in the winter, you do not need to hire a landscaper for the entire season (assuming you are able to perform light work). You could hire someone to remove leaves the first time, for example to get the bulk of the work done, and then you can rake remaining leaves that fall. When it snows, you can also save money by shoveling your own driveway, and when you get perhaps a foot or more of snow, you can hire an 'on-demand' snow blowing and shoveling service that may charge in the range of $20-30. This can also save you money versus the cost of buying and maintaining a snow blower, especially if it would likely not be used often.

Buy Mid-Tier Brand Items and Services

While you may save money by buying lower-tier (cheaper) items, they are generally lower quality. You also want to avoid buying expensive items, as it will quickly 'break the bank'.

Think long-term. If you buy cheap, you spend more in the long-term as you may need to replace something more often. For example, cheaper computers may have dated technology and will quickly become outdated. This also makes resale more challenging when you want to upgrade later.

You should be careful about buying 'on sale' or 'manager specials' because the quality may be inferior, or there may be damage, missing parts, etc. The demand may not be great.

There are exceptions to the rule, however. Some brands such as Coach build very long-lasting products using quality parts. Their items tend to last longer, and also have good resale value when sold on the secondhand market.

It is okay to buy slightly expensive items as one-off gifts for others, such as for Christmas, a gift for a client, etc. (if you can afford them).

Regarding contractors and services, do not always go for the lowest price/bid. I once saw a meme that resonated well – it showed a house being built by a contractor charging the lowest amount of money, and before it could be finished, it fell apart. There is a reason why experienced contractors charge more – you are buying confidence and peace of mind.

CREDIT SCORE ENHANCEMENTS

Typically, the higher your credit score is, the better your rate is to borrow money on a loan, which equates to greater savings long-term. The lower rate is an incentive for good (low-risk) borrowers to borrow money.

While the path to earning a high credit score is long and complex, generally this requires:

- Having a minimal amount of revolving, unsecured credit.

- Borrowing a limited amount of credit, compared to what your maximum borrowing amount is.

- Paying bills on time.

- Typically, not closing old credit cards, since you are measured by how long you have kept accounts open for.

LOANS

While borrowing at a variable rate may be lower than a fixed rate, a fixed rate gives you greater peace of mind knowing that your monthly amount due will be consistent. As a result, it makes it easier to budget and plan around. This is especially true when borrowing large amounts of money, either in the form of a personal loan, or a home equity line of credit (HELOC).

If loan payments get out of hand, see the Debt Consolidation and Repayment Programs section of this book.

DEALING WITH CUSTOMER SERVICE

If for example, your cable TV bill increases and you want to save money, call the provider's customer service or customer retention department. Ask how you can save money without dropping features or services. If first-line support does not give you the answer you are looking for (i.e. saying 'no'), ask to talk to their supervisor. Be careful not to ask to talk to a manager, because support is sometimes considered account management and they may just pass the phone to a coworker with the same rights and responsibilities they have.

When you ask to talk to a supervisor, support may suggest that they will say the same thing. They are trained to 'say no' and are pressured to not forward calls on to management. They may place you on hold and then suggest management is busy (this is generally a ploy to still not talk to management). At this point, firmly stress that you want to talk to their manager immediately. Usually they will, and sometimes management may actually be busy and they will need to call you later.

Keep in mind that the entire conversation is likely being recorded, so keep your tone in check, and also 'keep your cool'. If you are irate, your request may be ignored or denied.

Sometimes, if you threaten to leave the service, only then can they do something to help you. If you need additional leverage, particularly in cases where you feel you have an erroneous charge, you can threaten negative reviews, a complaint to the Better Business Bureau (BBB), sharing your situation on social media, filing a complaint with a license board (if the person is licensed), escalating to management that you find on LinkedIn, etc.

Do It Yourself

The Internet is full of 'do it yourself' training, and home improvement stores are also well-known to offer free or low-cost training for small or medium-sized projects.

YouTube is a great resource for learning tasks that you can do yourself to save money.

It may take some trial and error to gain experience and confidence when you do things yourself, versus hiring someone else. But you will notice the impact on your wallet, and only trade a bit of your own time. The other benefit is that you can have things done on your own terms and schedule. Depending on the task, you may also get some exercise value (i.e. landscaping).

Some common examples of people performing tasks themselves are:

- Haircuts. This can save you $20-30 a month (common range for a base haircut with tip). Have someone 'supervise' or monitor your haircutting skills from various angles while you hold a mirror to see how it goes the first time.

- Shoveling snow/snow-blowing, raking/blowing leaves.

If you are used to doing things yourself, and for some reason can no longer do so, you can look into charitable programs that help the elderly or disabled with common tasks for free or low cost.

LEARN TO SAY NO

Be wary of moochers. It is never good to have family, friends, or coworkers constantly asking for money, or expecting things for free. You are not the bank. If you give money, even on occasion, you will likely be asked again. History tells many that whenever you 'borrow' money, it is seldom seen again, despite someone's promise to do so. Although someone may be in a difficult situation, if the trend continues, questions need to be asked about why (if it is something that they can realistically change). Remember that even if someone is in a difficult situation, you may very well be as well. Point them in various directions to help, but say you are not in a position to give them money.

BEST TIME TO BUY

The higher the demand, and shorter the supply, the more something costs. If you buy when demand is low, and supply is high, you can save money.

Buying a new car for example is popular earlier in the year when people do not want to spend money right after spending money on Christmas gifts, and are also waiting for their annual bonuses and tax returns in the spring.

Some exceptions to the rule are when all companies compete for consumer spending on Black Friday (Friday following Thanksgiving in the US), and Cyber Monday (the Monday following). But some vendors have been known to offer the same product, but a different model with cheaper or lesser-quality components to make the product appeal to more people, while increasing the profit for the seller. Just keep this in mind when buying and read the product description, take note of the part references and product model number, and read the reviews.

CAR BUYING

As stated previously, you do not need a luxury-edition car with leather seats, alloy wheels, etc. Premium features are generally pure profit due to the high profit margins with these materials. You can always add premium features for less money after you buy a car, if you have a capable/licensed auto mechanic do the work.

The old adage that you get 'more car' from a base model, non-luxury car is true. Sometimes features and capabilities in a less expensive car outperform more expensive luxury cars. Luxury car advertising and brand management can be very expensive, and they need to pass costs on to the consumer.

Beyond noting the 'best time to buy' information in the prior section, you can save more money by asking for a price of a car that has been on the lot for a while (this information may be on the dealership's website listing). You can also try asking for the best price of a car in a less desirable color, and then asking for the same price for a car color you like.

Never tell the salesperson what your budget is, what you do for work, or what you want your monthly payment to be. If you want to buy, buy – do not be forced into a lease deal, which many dealerships are pushing now, even if they claim they typically no longer sell outright due to their business model. They are just trying to push you towards areas where they get more profit (their interests, not yours).

INSURANCE

Of course, if you have insurance, you can save a considerable amount of money compared to if you did not and something happened. You can generally only get insurance ahead of something happening, not for something that already happened.

Insurance can also protect you from lawsuits and give you more peace of mind. Talk to an insurance agent to learn more.

Be careful if your state does not require car insurance. That places a significant liability on you, and you could be forced to pay very high medical and property damage bills if you are not covered.

BEING FRUGAL

It is okay if others consider you "cheap".

Do not be afraid to say no to company lunches, dinners, or drinks where you are expected to pay out of pocket (but show up at least once in a while to let others know you have not 'checked out' and are still part of the team – some may take it personally).

Being frugal does not mean doing everything (including fixing things) yourself. There are countless safety, operability, and mechanical optimization impacts to consider. Sometimes for peace of mind (and considering the value of your time), it is well worth hiring a specialist from a reputable company in your area.

As part of being frugal, you should avoid frequent expensive vacations. Try to take time off and spend it locally, as this helps avoid the need to spend money on hotels and eating out (with a tip impact). There are plenty of local opportunities where you can see wildlife, take photos, eat at restaurants more cheaply, etc. Tourist areas always demand higher prices.

SAVE MONEY BY BEING PROACTIVE WITH PREVENTATIVE MAINTENANCE

It definitely pays off in the long term to make proactive purchases to avoid issues later on. Common examples are to replace 'mission critical' appliances such as water heaters, furnaces, and air conditioning before they fail. There is the crowd that subscribes to the 'if it is not broken, do not fix it' approach, which is fine to an extent, but if you are within a certain recommended threshold for an appliance's lifetime, you are gambling somewhat. It is better to be safe than sorry, again for peace of mind. Hiring inspectors to review appliances can help prolong the life of something, but you have to weigh the cost of hiring the inspector, and also consider that they cannot see everything (or if they can, they may not notice in lieu of other checklist items and time restraints between other appointments). You can never place full trust in someone servicing your home, and it is worth researching on your own and asking questions, preferably with multiple vendors to aid with decision making.

You should never pay for an assessment of whether you should upgrade – many vendors offer free estimates. This should not be a paid aspect of a plumbing or HVAC visit (for example), unless they notice things while performing other work and suggest work done. You can call the company afterwards to send someone for the no-cost assessment to get a better idea of scope and cost. Always confirm whether work is required by getting more than one quote/estimate, preferably from 2-3 other vendors.

You should also never hold off on regular maintenance (preferably done by a specialist), which applies to all major appliances, even if it is as simple as clearing lint/dust from a filter, cleaning, etc. Your home should be a priority. Safety concerns can also arise if maintenance is not performed, to include dirty water from rusted water tanks to carbon monoxide from a furnace, etc.

Beyond home appliances, a home inspector can help identify other issues such as end-of-life roof shingles, leaks, cracks in the basement that need attention, radon issues, structural integrity of a deck, etc. Make sure you prioritize these issues because they can get worse fast, and you end up spending more money in the long-run. There is also the cosmetic aspect – no one wants to see a derelict deck, driveway, sidewalk, etc. Fixing issues ASAP also frees you from liability issues, especially damaged border walls/fences if the neighbor has children or pets.

Home inspectors are never just limited to when you buy your home. They can be valuable in identifying issues you are not aware of, whether it be 5, 10, or more years later.

Being proactive versus reactive is always best.

CERTIFICATIONS

Keep in mind that virtually anyone/any company can offer a certification. In other words, I can set up course 'A' and offer certification 'B' after you complete it with a pass/fail test, or after you earn a minimum score. And then charge an annual renewal fee.

Well-known companies make their courses more recognized/reputable in target industries by involving professors and industry/thought leaders, and then marketing the course value/return on investment (ROI).

Some certifications are well recognized, and are very difficult to achieve, requiring many hours of study and preparation.

Some industries, such as real estate, have countless certifications that are not widely recognized, and consumers may not know about them (or care). The bottom line for many is whether you can effectively perform a service or deliver a quality product.

If you have certifications, or are thinking about investing in them, consider renewal costs and time required to prepare for continuing education. You should also consider whether you will get reimbursed for any course, test, initial certification, or renewal costs.

Consider whether it makes sense for you to get certified and maintain the certification. If consumers/end users do not care, perhaps it is an incentive within your industry when making new connections (it may help open new doors/opportunities). If there is little value, drop the certification, and you can save potentially hundreds of dollars a year.

If you do see value in a certification, keep an eye out for renewal deadlines and continuing education requirements. You do not want an administrative cancellation for forgetting to renew.

HOME COST

If you become a licensed real estate salesperson or broker, you can save money when you buy or sell your own home (provided you are not under contract with another agent). You just need to make sure that if you only have a salesperson license, that you have a broker to sponsor you (check your state/territory laws/regulations on this). You will likely need to disclose that you are a licensed real estate agent when making an offer, to support consumer protection laws.

To save more money, you can target properties that have a small house with no garage, but a large lot (i.e. at least half an acre). This allows you to build an extension catered to your preferences, which can be done whenever it best suits you financially.

As stated previously, avoid buying large homes, especially mansions. It is not uncommon for people who buy these homes to not live in them year-round, and they may visit for a few months or maybe weeks at a time. This is not conducive to savings goals, especially with a large mortgage payment and ongoing taxes.

PREPARE YOUR OWN FOOD WHERE POSSIBLE

When you make your own food, it is generally healthier compared to what restaurants offer (usually high in salt content, to upsell drinks where most of their profit is derived from). Restaurant food may also be high in fat/calories.

Simple fixed meals can help encourage this practice. Plenty of cookbooks are available online, and local courses offered at restaurants can help. The latter can also be a good networking opportunity.

It is also worth brewing your own coffee/tea. K-Cups are a good alternative, but not the most environmentally friendly option since the pods need to be thrown out after every serving. By preparing your own coffee/tea, you save perhaps $3-5/drink every day.

DROPPING SERVICES AND SUBSCRIPTIONS

Some services are bloated with various features or shows/stations that are never used/watched/listened to. Consider whether you can live without them, especially with sky-high costs. Many streaming services start at $20-40+ per month, and cable TV bundles can run anywhere from $150-250/month.

To break from cable TV, consider using antennas where they are legal for free TV. (The channels will be limited and you may not get them in HD quality, however.)

Internet plans are making it easier to break from traditional cable TV plans. YouTube for example has many free videos, if you do not mind listening to occasional ads. Or you can upgrade to premium service and not have to listen to the ads.

It is worth calling your cable provider from time to time (at least once a year) to see what their current promotions are. There is typically no need to decrease/remove channels if you are just looking to keep your current cost consistent, versus seeing the cost go up after your initial promotion period ends.

Music is also 'free' if you listen to songs on the radio.

Libraries are unfortunately often overlooked in today's digital world. But they offer books and e-books for free rentals to in-town/city residences, including free or low-cost rentals of movies and music. Newspapers and magazines can also be checked out. Some libraries offer free e-book rentals without requiring a trip to the library.

Consider whether you may be overpaying if a service you currently pay for (separately) is bundled with another service (i.e. cable TV). You can cancel and absorb savings that way. For example, instead of paying for Netflix separately, Comcast may include Netflix in some plans.

You may also be able to save money from monthly TV box rentals in other rooms if you buy a Roku TV device and use the cable TV application (if offered in your area). Comcast, for example, offers an application on Roku, which negates the need to spend money on monthly TV box rentals.

Of course, do not cut back on anything necessary such as home security monitoring, medical monitoring, etc. Those all fall within the 'need' category and should be retained.

See if you can get the same (or similar) content from paid newspaper and magazine subscriptions for free on the Internet.

For cloud software products, you may be able to find alternative open-source software that performs the same tasks. This is a bit difficult for vendors with proprietary formats with deep industry roots (i.e. Photoshop in the creative/media industry). But you do have some viable options here. You just have to weigh pros and cons such as availability of support, etc.

You can potentially also cut back on cloud storage costs if you set up an in-home cloud storage device on your network. There are many options available on Amazon's site (Western Digital's cloud drive products, for example). The downside of this is that you do not have a backup in the event of a fire or theft. But you can configure automatic cloud backups of specific files and folders as needed. Amazon, Microsoft, Google, and Dropbox have solid cloud backup options, if you want to review them. When evaluating cloud storage options, consider compliance and certifications, and where your data will physically reside (i.e. in the US, or overseas).

BUY USED OR SECONDHAND

Buy gently used where possible/practical. This helps avoid depreciation, and allows you to sell for roughly the same cost you purchased an item for later on.

Popular places to do this include:

- Estate sales - advertised on EstateSales.net and EstateSales.org.

- Yard sales.

- Online marketplaces such as eBay, Facebook Marketplace, or Craigslist.

Sometimes vendors allow you to test-drive/trial used products before committing. If you do this, clarify whether a potential return is buyer paid, or seller paid.

DEBT CONSOLIDATION AND REPAYMENT PROGRAMS

Fortunately, programs exist to help you consolidate your debt and/or repay debt for a lower rate with smaller fixed payments (typically for unsecured debt only, which includes credit card debt and personal loan debt). Participating in these programs can affect your credit score, however, since a comment may be added indicating that you are in a consolidation/repayment program. This appears negative to lenders, because (without knowing you), it appears as if you cannot manage debt on your own, and the weight of this program is just below going bankrupt. Some mortgage/lending applications ask if you have participated in one of these programs within 'x' amount of time.

Aside from this, if the program helps you, it may be worth pursuing this option. The challenge is finding a reputable *nonprofit* company, as there are many scammers, or companies charging high fees, even under the guise of a nonprofit organization. Your fee should be minimal, if any, as the third-party lenders typically pay the debt consolidation/repayment company to assist consumers.

Do not be afraid to call the loan administrator/customer service directly (not going through a consolidation/repayment company). This is called an 'in-house' option. There is less paperwork, and if you explain your situation (while being honest), they will likely help.

NEW MORTGAGES AND REFINANCING EXISTING LOANS

You can realize long-term savings by buying 'points' when buying a mortgage initially or refinancing.

You can also ask for the bank, credit union, or mortgage broker to lock a rate, and ask to absorb any lower rates they see within the rate lock window.

After you get an initial mortgage, you may find that rates drop considerably. It is usually worth refinancing if the rate drops by at least a full point, and you plan on staying in the home long-term (for example 5-10 years or more).

If you do pursue refinancing, it may be tempting to refinance to 15 years or lower. But consider unforeseen circumstances/events that might cause interruptions in your income. Can you afford the higher payment long-term? No one knows. You can optionally make higher payments to save long-term, which provides more flexibility.

Talk with a mortgage agent/broker to determine your break-even point and see if refinancing is worth it. Consider closing costs, appraisal costs, and monthly savings. It is important to speak with agents who do not make you feel rushed and who give you the sense that they want to help you. If they sound busy, give short answers, ask you to apply for a mortgage over the phone (which would be a hard credit report pull and could affect your credit score), find someone else. There are many good agents out there.

You might want to consider getting a second mortgage (i.e. HELOC) versus refinancing with a cash-out option. Mortgage terms are typically long, and HELOC loans usually have a 10-year repayment period. The shorter the repayment period, generally the less interest you pay. You may also get a better rate with a HELOC, versus with a mortgage.

On the topic of refinancing mortgages, it may also be worth refinancing student loans to save even more money.

TRADING AND MAKING BARTER DEALS

Another way to save is to trade products and services, or make barter deals.

For example, you can offer to paint or repair your landlord's apartment building in exchange for reduced rent. Or you can offer to build a website, or offer handcrafted items in exchange for products and services (sometimes showing them a portfolio while highlighting the market value of the trade is helpful). With the website example, you can potentially make money after the deal by maintaining and supporting the site.

Approaching people with these offers may make you come across as desperate. But not everyone will see the offer that way. They may see you as entrepreneurial and motivated, and be willing to listen and find value in your offer.

LOWER COST OF LIVING

Living somewhere that has a lower cost of living can also help you save money. Particularly in areas that do not have sales tax, or areas with no state income tax. Some areas get hit very hard with state and local (i.e. city) taxes, in addition to federal taxes and high housing expenses.

It is possible to commute from areas that have a lower cost of living to areas that pay more (bubbles). Many people do this, but you would need to be okay with more traffic and time spent driving to/from where you work. You may also be able to adjust your schedule by getting to work early, but that does not necessarily mean you can always leave earlier due to work demands and issues that come up (unless your team is understanding and respects that you come in earlier). Just be sure not to take 2-hour lunches.

Preferably, you should target areas with a lower cost of living that allow you to work remotely full-time, or at least part-time. Make sure that these jobs do not lower your pay based on where you live, as that will defeat the purpose.

COST COMPARISON/COUPON SAVINGS

Cost comparison and coupon saving sites are very helpful tools to identify vendors offering similar products for less. They can also communicate if the current price is higher or lower than the average price (denoting whether it is the best time to buy).

Use product codes from the manufacturer when comparison shopping, and not the vendor product code, which is different.

A service called Honey (https://www.joinhoney.com/ref/haerix) offers a browser plugin that automatically enters promotion codes on checkout pages. It saves you money then, and you also earn points to redeem for gift cards.

Other coupon sites allow you to print coupons for the store, or download/claim digital coupons that you can show cashiers on your phone. Some companies are 'old school' and still require print coupons, but digital coupon redemption is becoming more popular as it is more eco-friendly.

Gas savings phone apps are also useful, as they can show you gas stations in the area with currently reported gas prices.

Credit card companies sometimes offer special deals on their website as well. You just have to login to your account and claim them. They get applied when you use the credit card at the vendors within the specified time frames. As an aside, you can take note of the credit card cash-back offers (i.e. 'x' percent at gas stations, 'y' percent at restaurants, etc.). If you pay your credit card balance off regularly, this can be a good deal.

Twitter users also tend to post promotion codes which you can use. Just be careful what links you click on, as some promotion codes are associated with affiliates/partners who earn money whenever you use their promotion code and they may trigger multiple windows.

RETURNS

You can generally return items that you bought without issue. Standard return windows range from 30-90 days. Sometimes the window is less, or even more, so check the return policy before buying.

Returning is a good option especially if you bought something on impulse and later regret the decision.

Even if something you bought is beyond the return window, as long as you have the receipt, many stores accept returns. The item needs to be in resalable condition, and they may still need to carry the product. If beyond the return window, the store typically offers store credit (never cash). But store credit, especially at stores that have been around for a while and where you shop regularly, is just as good as cash. As long as you are within policy, you should not have any trouble returning an item and can always reference return policy and ask for management if a return is refused. Reputable companies always make it easy to return items, since it is part of their customer service/satisfaction goals.

Beware of long return windows, because it is easy to forget to return something (companies know this when they set the long periods of time). But you can still try to negotiate store credit in these cases.

EVENTS

If you need to host an event, you might be able to negotiate paying a cost in the form of a donation if the event will be hosted at a historic venue. Talk to the event director at the venue and your tax/financial advisor for more information.

INVESTMENT OPPORTUNITIES

"Never depend on single income. Make investment to create a second
source." –*Warren Buffett*
(Goodreads[3], n.d.)

This section is intentionally being kept short. I want to reiterate that I
am not an investment consultant or financial advisor. It is meant to
provide basic information that you can potentially leverage with
specialists.

Recall that in this book's Introduction, I shared a Chinese proverb that
stated: "The best time to plant a tree was 20 years ago. The second
best time is now." (Caporicci, 2020). You are always in a good position
to start investing; even if it is not much now, you can still earn money
on whatever you can afford to invest. Once you get to a certain point,
saving and investing becomes easier as you can appreciate the impact
it has.

You can put money in high-yield funds, or the stock market. A popular
investment path is investing in low-fee index funds (such as those
offered by Vanguard).

Take into account that splurging on things and making frivolous
purchases takes away from future earning potential. A $100 item
purchased 10 years ago that now collects dust could have translated to
$5,000 or more with the power of compounding.

Do not cash out a 401(k) or other investments unless absolutely
necessary. You will have to pay a penalty if you do this before
retirement age, and you will regret the decision later in life. Even if you

borrow from your 401(k) and later repay what you borrowed, you still lose out on compounding interest.

Never collect things as an investment. There are some uncommon ways to invest such as buying rare stamps, rare sports cards, rare art, etc., but you need to hold on to these for a very long time. These are also best sold at big-name auction companies (i.e. Sotheby's, Christie's, etc.) and carry high fees.

Avoid investing in gold and silver. These are considered 'hedge' investments that do well in bad economic conditions or tense conditions that may lead to war, but precious metal is difficult to move/sell.

You should also not invest in risky investments such as Bitcoin since the price fluctuates too much. If you need to access money, you could potentially lose a lot of money. Bitcoin and digital currency trading sites are also targets for hackers, and many people have lost their investments this way due to minimal regulation and consumer protections.

When playing the stock market, make sure you research your stock choices. Diversify your investments (preferably in multiple industries) and do not put 'all your eggs in the same basket'. Do not follow others with investments, as by the time you follow, someone else is already very rich and you are trailing behind.

Roth IRA investments can be a good option to pay taxes upfront when you make investments, versus later on when you draw.

JOB SEARCHING

"You get paid in direct proportion to the difficulty of problems you solve." –*Elon Musk*
(Goodreads[1], n.d.)

The more you think, the more you generally get paid.

When looking for a new job, know that once you start working for a new employer, it is difficult to get a salary increase or move up. You should negotiate the best terms, position, and salary possible. Research the market and what others get paid at the company (from Glassdoor, for example). HR may ask you what your salary expectations are, but they cannot ask what your current salary is in most areas now. The way around this is to say that it depends on many factors, and that you like to look at the entire package including benefits. Immediately after, politely inquire if you may ask what the budgeted starting range is. From there you can let them know if your expectations are in line with what they claim to pay.

Cash is always king with any offer. Bonuses and benefits are nice (always get everything in writing), but the latter are generally discretionary, meaning a company can adjust bonuses and benefits at will. They can do the same with your salary in at-will states.

Make sure that you are happy with the offer. Know your worth, and consider your debt payoff goals when making a new move, especially after 3+ years at a company. Try targeting at least a 10% increase at a minimum. Job moves, and salary bumps that come with them, are typically the fastest way to pay off debt. You cannot necessarily count on small additive measures alone (i.e. not buying coffee, not going out to restaurants, etc.), and business ventures are not always successful.

Always pursue your job search discreetly. Do not threaten to find another job or even say that you are unhappy with conditions. This will likely work against you and the company may start making you redundant and potentially replace you later.

There are pros and cons with starting a new job.

A good amount of time is spent updating your resume and portfolio, applying, and preparing for interviews. Some interviews may require additional time if you are asked to prepare a presentation or a small project.

Once hired for the new job, you then have to build new relationships, and typically put in more hours to learn the new company's tools and processes, market and competition, and products and services. Adjusting to a new culture is difficult as well, especially if you are used to working remotely more often, need to adjust to answering and making phone calls more often, or are dealing with a longer commute, etc. Some cultures even involve 'workaholic' types, with competition of who gets to the office first and stays latest, who skips lunch to work, etc. You have to be careful. Luckily, there are plenty of review sites out there (i.e. Glassdoor) that can help you make a more qualified decision.

If you are lucky, you are hired for a senior role. But sometimes, especially for entry-level roles, you have to start from the beginning... and that sometimes means doing the work that other people who have been there longer do not especially like.

Sometimes job searching is needed if you find out about potential restructuring, reduction, or ramp-down plans (corporate layoff terms). State WARN (Worker Adjustment and Retraining Notification) notices help employees plan ahead if layoff plans are not necessarily announced by your employer. You can also attend or listen to/read quarterly investor calls, and search for anonymous layoff rumor discussions online – there are dedicated sites for layoff reports and discussions. If you listen to the investor calls or read the transcripts, look for subtle hints including executive tones and responses. It is best not to discuss layoffs with coworkers. If you are approached by someone, just keep the discussion high-level and sympathize with them, but do not share specific thoughts as that may fuel the rumor mill and someone else may claim you said or heard something, etc.

When it is time to resign from your current job, try to do so after you collect your annual bonus. It would be a big loss to forfeit a 10% target bonus, for example, if you had to move on to a new job one month before you received the bonus. If needed, you can try to negotiate a signing bonus with your new employer while explaining that you will be forfeiting the bonus from your current employer, if you cannot wait to join after receiving the bonus.

···  ···

ENHANCING YOUR VALUE AND REPUTATION AT YOUR PRESENT JOB

Sometimes, especially at larger companies, you can try to move to other areas, or accept more responsibilities in your current team/division.

Having an interest in learning about various topics, even if not directly related to what you do, will make you more valuable to others. They may start asking you more questions, and management will notice. You will also be able to offer advice and suggestions to improve products and processes with a greater understanding of the business.

Instead of being an entrepreneur, an intrapreneur is someone within a company that contributes ideas to make the company more profitable. This requires 'people skills' to pitch ideas and win support, but is not difficult to do.

Your reputation matters with everything at work. Consider everything you do to be a 'test', and do not burn bridges. Keep your ego in check, and do not come across as arrogant. High performers may carry an 'I am more important than you' attitude and get away with a lot, because of their value to the company (managers are hard-pressed to do anything). But by following this, they further drive an independent contributor brand, and will likely not be asked to assume a leadership role as a result. Of course there are exceptions, but smart companies know better to place the right people in the right roles.

Always exert confidence when you talk, carry a 'can-do' attitude, and offer support for others. Try to absorb material quickly, and even if you come to work with a bad attitude, never lose your temper. Apologize when you do blow off steam, and always offer solutions rather than complain or simply state issues that require resolution. That is what your boss hired you to do.

Never despise others' success if they get promoted versus you. Congratulate them, and aspire to be like them. Be patient, and you will likely be offered a role later. Just be sure to express interest, make yourself/your work visible to decision makers, and do not be afraid to keep checking in for new roles, even if they are not posted. It is not uncommon for people to be placed in unposted positions (even not posted internally).

Always get your work done with high quality. Dress appropriately for business ('dress for success' concept). Even if you work in engineering/software/IT for example, where wearing blue jeans and sneakers is common, dressing up separates you from others and shows that you go the extra mile.

You should also look into training and certifications. You can learn more about the company's products by participating in training sessions in your own time (if it cannot be sponsored during the work day). If training outside work (for a certification, for example) cannot be reimbursed by your employer, you can still pursue the training on your own time (i.e. a week off using vacation time), and you will have a step up from other coworkers as a result. Just be sure you pay attention, absorb the material, and ask questions. If you are not 100% focused/vested in learning, you will never get 100% value.

··· ❼ ···

ADDITIONAL INCOME STREAMS

This line from the movie *Horrible Bosses* may resonate with some:

"I own you... don't walk around here thinking you have free will, because you don't. I could crush you anytime I want." *–Spoken by the fictional character Dave Harken in the movie "Horrible Bosses."* (Horrible Bosses Quotes, n.d.)

If you do not like your boss, he/she probably does not like you either. In employment at will states, you can be dismissed for any reason, at any time.

You never want to be at someone else's disposal. To protect yourself and your family, you should pursue additional income opportunities.

When you consider this, never go into business with friends and family.

Some ideas for additional income include:

- Renting a room in your house.

- Starting a side job, preferably something that you naturally gravitate toward, since it would be something you do on your own time nights and weekends.

- Creative pursuits such as art and photography, which you can sell online (eBay, etc.)

- Selling unnecessary items collecting dust in your own home, or in storage.

If you can automate the business, that is even better. Typically, this can be done online using 'turnkey' solutions that can attract new business through advertising. But there is also a lot of competition, and you will need to find the right niches to be successful. An excellent quote from Warren Buffett expresses the automation goal very well: "If you don't find a way to make money while you sleep, you will work until you die." (Self Made Success, 2019).

Service businesses are preferable, since they do not require any inventory which can be a hassle to store, move to make room for new inventory, and ship. Service businesses are generally lower-risk as well. With that said, you can always create prototypes and start with limited inventory to see what the demand/reception is and then scale up.

For faster success, you can pitch your idea with others and partner with them. Focus on people who have experience and a track record of success in the same industry. Sign non-disclosure agreements to protect your idea, and always put everything in writing that you agree to, even if over email (but preferably in signed contract form). You can do this easily by suggesting you just want to do it as a formality to make sure you are on the same page with expectations and understandings.

Never leave your current job to start a new business. In a perfect world, you can keep your current job that likely offers a better deal on health, dental, and life insurance… in addition to supplemental income in the form of a part-time job on the side. But there may come a time when you start earning a consistent revenue stream with your side business and the income becomes similar. From there, you may need to make a cost/benefit decision, inclusive of weighing stress/happiness/enjoyment of life, and choose to pursue your side business full-time.

TOOLS AND PROCESSES

I use a Google Spreadsheet to maintain my checkbook, monitor debt, and check my net worth. I created a copy of this for you to use, which can be accessed via: https://www.terminatedebt.com/tools/.

All of the values of course reflect temporary, fictitious data. You can modify the data and templates to best suit your needs.

The checkbook register allows you to track previous transactions, in addition to future charges to budget accordingly.

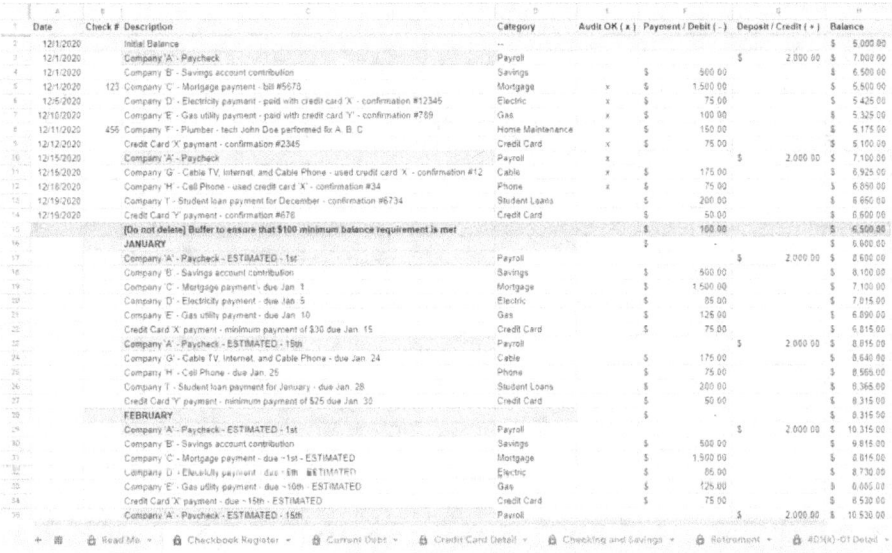

Various charts and graphs are also included in other areas of the spreadsheet.

A total debt pie chart, which shows you the percentage of debt within specified categories.

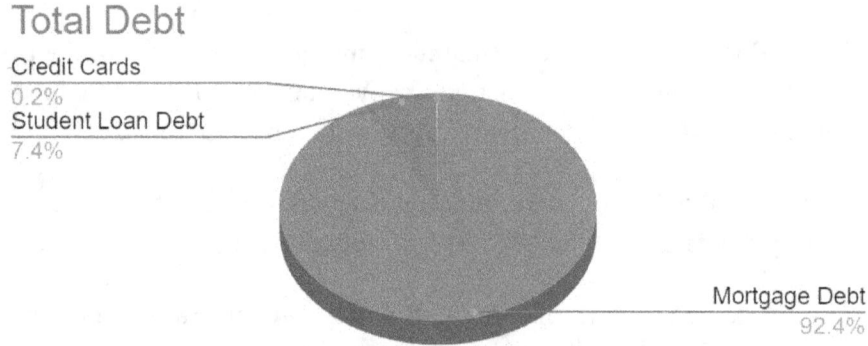

A line graph showing credit card debt over the course of one or two years to track payoff progress. It also helps you identify periods of higher spending, to help control future spending.

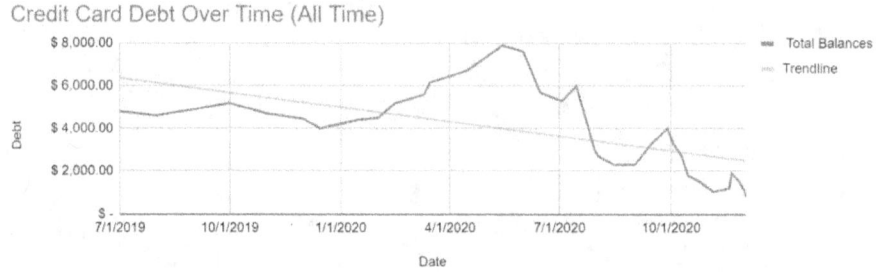

The value of your investments can also be tracked, to help you get a sense of how compounding interest is working for you, and whether you should start investing more to take advantage of potentially higher returns.

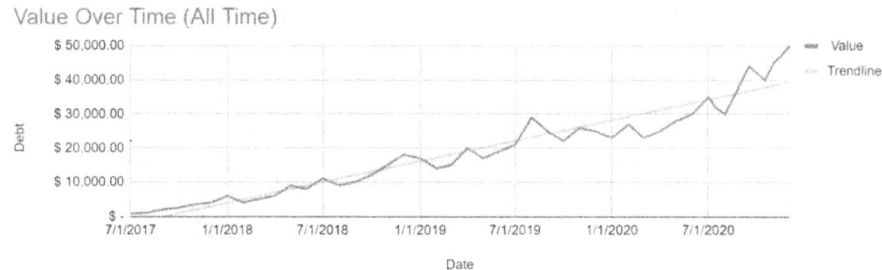

Towards the end of the spreadsheet, you will find a net worth assessment. On this sheet, you can copy your total debt, and list all of your assets. The spreadsheet will calculate the totals and present your current net worth.

Net Worth

Net Worth				$	350,300.00
Debt				**$**	**270,500.00**
Description		Amount	Comments		Balance Last Checked
Total from "Current Debt" tab		$ 270,500.00			12/2/2020
Assets				**$**	**620,800.00**
Description		Amount	Comments		Balance Last Checked
Appraised value of home		$ 400,000.00	Appraised by __ on date __		
Car		$ 4,000.00	Conservative estimate as per __		12/2/2020
Checking and savings (see "Checking and Savings" tab)		$ 11,000.00			12/2/2020
Stock market (not including retirement funds)		$ 5,000.00			12/2/2020
Retirement funds (see "Retirement" tab)		$ 195,000.00			12/2/2020
Personal possessions - general home goods (non antiques)		$ 2,000.00	Conservative estimate		
Personal possessions - general home goods (antiques)		$ 1,500.00	Conservative estimate		
Personal possessions - coins / silver bullion		$ 1,000.00	Conservative estimate		
Personal possessions - books		$ 100.00	Conservative estimate		
Personal possessions - oil paintings, prints, etc.		$ 500.00	Conservative estimate		
Personal possessions - tools, lawn mower, yard cart		$ 200.00	Conservative estimate		
Personal possessions - computer/office equipment and supplies		$ 300.00	Conservative estimate		
Personal possessions - misc. other collectables		$ 200.00	Conservative estimate		

Feel free to create a copy of the spreadsheet and use it. I added notes throughout the spreadsheet to explain how you can use the various sheets. Only a basic working knowledge of spreadsheets such as Excel is required to use this.

For other tools, you may be interested in creating a Google Calendar to track all of your meetings and tasks. You can have the calendar send you reminders to pay debt for example. If you want an online reminder, you can use a notebook or day planner, which will also help you feel less overwhelmed.

When applying for loans, you may find value in using this payment calculator, to give you a better idea of monthly payments: https://www.calculator.net/payment-calculator.html

··· ···

CONCLUSION

"May the force be with you." *–First spoken by the fictional character Obi-Wan Kenobi in the movie "Star Wars: Episode IV A New Hope."* (Fandom, n.d.)

I hope that you found this book useful. I attempted to address a true 360-degree overview of debt strategies to help people with various debt conditions. Remember that the most valuable asset is your will to improve – stay motivated, and know that there truly is light at the end of the tunnel. Once you get out of debt, you will feel less stressed, and feel more 'free' in day-to-day life.

After eliminating debt, emphasis should be put on building a healthy savings account, but do not go to extreme measures where the only thing you care about is money. Remember that older generations consider wealth to be equally important as health. Focus on happiness and meaningful pursuits.

REFERENCES

Caporicci, B. (n.d.). *The best time to plant a tree was 20 years ago ... what this Chinese Proverb means to you now*. Retrieved from https://getsproutstudio.com/plant-a-tree/

Fandom. (n.d.). *May the Force be with you*. Retrieved from https://starwars.fandom.com/wiki/May_the_Force_be_with_y ou

Goodreads[1]. (n.d.). *Quote by Elon Musk*. Retrieved from https://www.goodreads.com/quotes/8389664-you-get-paid-in-direct-proportion-to-the-difficulty-of

Goodreads[2]. (n.d.). *Quote by Emma Hart*. Retrieved from https://www.goodreads.com/quotes/824321-just-because-you-can-t-see-something-doesn-t-mean-it-isn-t

Goodreads[3]. (n.d.). *Quote by Warren Buffett*. Retrieved from https://www.goodreads.com/quotes/7374466-never-depend-on-single-income-make-investment-to-create-a

IMDB. (n.d.) *Indiana Jones and the Last Crusade (1989) - Robert Eddison: Grail Knight*. Retrieved from https://www.imdb.com/title/tt0097576/characters/nm0248 848

Horrible Bosses Quotes. (n.d.) *Horrible Bosses Quotes*. Retrieved from https://www.moviequotesandmore.com/horrible-bosses-quotes/

Lyrics. (n.d.). *Material Girl Lyrics*. Retrieved from https://www.lyrics.com/lyric/26538387/Madonna/Material+ Girl

PsychCentral. (2017, May 30). *The Only Constant Is Change*. Retrieved from https://psychcentral.com/lib/the-only-constant-is-change

Quote Investigator[1]. (2016, Aug. 18). *It Is Not the Mountain We Conquer, But Ourselves*. Retrieved from https://quoteinvestigator.com/2016/08/18/conquer/

Quote Investigator[2]. (2015, Jul. 23). *With Great Power Comes Great Responsibility*. Retrieved from https://quoteinvestigator.com/2015/07/23/great-power/

Ronald Reagan Presidential Library & Museum. (1987, Dec. 8). *Remarks on Signing the Intermediate-Range Nuclear Forces Treaty*. Retrieved from https://www.reaganlibrary.gov/archives/speech/remarks-signing-intermediate-range-nuclear-forces-treaty

Self Made Success. (2019, May 31). *If You Don't Find a Way to Make Money While You Sleep...* Retrieved from https://selfmadesuccess.com/make-money-sleep-warren-buffett/

Society for the Protection of New Hampshire Forests. (n.d.). *Madame Sherri Forest*. Retrieved from https://forestsociety.org/property/madame-sherri-forest

The X-Files Transcripts Archive[1]. (n.d.). *X-Files Season 2, Episode "Little Green Men", Scene 18, Deep Throat*. Retrieved from http://www.insidethex.co.uk/transcrp/scrp201.htm

The X-Files Transcripts Archive[2]. (n.d.). *X-Files Season 5, Episode "The End", Scene 12, Cigarette Smoking Man*. Retrieved from http://www.insidethex.co.uk/transcrp/scrp520.htm

CREDITS

Cover photo by Simon Migaj -
    https://www.pexels.com/photo/person-stands-on-snow-covered-mountain-looking-at-fireworks-767172/

CREDITS

ABOUT THE AUTHOR

Curtis Carmichael holds an MS in Information Technology from Southern New Hampshire University, a BS in Web Management and Internet Commerce, and an English minor from Plymouth State University. He currently lives in southern New Hampshire.